Understanding 365/Azure for Everyone

CHATGPT4o with j. p. ames

© Copyright 2024, j. p. ames. All rights reserved.

Understanding 365/Azure for Everyone

Unlock the Full Potential of Cloud Services with Ease!

Are you a manager or IT professional looking to streamline your organization's operations with Microsoft 365 and Azure? "Understanding 365/Azure for Everyone" is your ultimate guide to mastering these powerful cloud services. Written in an accessible style, this comprehensive book breaks down complex concepts into simple, easy-to-understand language, making it perfect for both beginners and experienced users.

What You'll Learn:

- **Microsoft 365 Essentials**: Discover how to set up and manage domains, email, and licenses.
- **Active Directory Integration**: Learn the benefits of integrating on-premises Active Directory with Azure AD for centralized management.
- **Security Best Practices**: Implement conditional access policies, multi-factor authentication (2FA), and other essential security measures.
- **Azure Virtual Machines and Storage**: Step-by-step guides on setting up and managing virtual servers and storage.
- **SharePoint vs. Traditional File Servers**: Understand why migrating to SharePoint can enhance security, accessibility, and productivity.
- **Teams for Collaboration**: Maximize your team's productivity with effective use of Microsoft Teams.
- **Power BI for Data Visualization**: Create interactive reports and dashboards to make data-driven decisions.
- **Networking and Security**: Learn to set up secure VPN connections and leverage SSLVPN for remote access.
- **Automation with Azure Functions**: Automate routine tasks and improve operational efficiency.
- **Case Studies and Best Practices**: Real-world examples and best practices to guide your implementation.

Equip yourself with the knowledge to leverage Microsoft 365 and Azure for your organization. Whether you're a manager, IT professional, or a business owner, this book provides the insights and tools you need to succeed in the modern digital workplace.

Congratulations on ordering your copy of "Understanding 365/Azure for Everyone" and taking the first step towards transforming your business with Microsoft's cloud solutions!

Table of Contents

Understanding 365/Azure for Everyone 1
Understanding 365/Azure for Everyone 2
   What You'll Learn: 2
Understanding 365/Azure for Everyone 5
   Chapter 1: Introduction to Microsoft 365 and Azure 5
      What are Microsoft 365 and Azure? 5
      Difference Between Microsoft 365 and Azure 5
      Real-World Use Case: Choosing Between Microsoft 365 and Azure 5
   Chapter 2: Setting Up Microsoft 365 6
      Domain Assignment 6
      Real-World Example: Setting Up Your Company's Email 6
   Chapter 3: Active Directory Integration 7
      What is Active Directory (AD)? 7
      Integration with Microsoft 365 and Azure AD 7
      Real-World Example: Centralized User Management 8
   Chapter 4: Conditional Access Policies 9
      What are Conditional Access Policies? 9
      How to Create and Manage Conditional Access Policies 9
      Real-World Example: Restricting Access Based on Location 10
   Chapter 5: Two-Factor Authentication (2FA) 11
      Integrating 2FA with Microsoft 365 11
      Setting Up 2FA with Duo and Other Providers 11
      Real-World Example: Securing User Accounts with 2FA 11
   Chapter 6: Mail and Licensing 12
      Setting Up and Managing Email 12
      Managing Licenses and Subscriptions 12
      Real-World Example: Allocating Licenses to Users 13
   Chapter 7: Virtual Servers and Storage in Azure 14
      Creating and Managing Virtual Servers 14
      Real-World Example: Hosting a Website on Azure 15
   Chapter 8: SharePoint and File Management 16
      Why Ditch a File Server for SharePoint? 16
      Real-World Example: Migrating Files to SharePoint 16
   Chapter 9: Teams and Collaboration 17
      Using Microsoft Teams for Collaboration 17
      Real-World Example: Organizing Team Communication and Projects 18
   Chapter 10: Power BI and Data Visualization 19
      Getting Started with Power BI 19
      Real-World Example: Visualizing Sales Data with Power BI 19
   Chapter 11: Networking and Security 20
      Local Networking Integration via IKE VPN 20
      Real-World Example: Securely Accessing Azure Resources from Your Local Network 21
   Chapter 12: Additional Crucial Features 22
      Other Important Features of Microsoft 365 and Azure 22

Real-World Example: Automating Routine Tasks with Azure Functions	23
Chapter 13: Case Studies and Best Practices	24
Real-World Case Studies	24
Best Practices for Implementation and Management	24
Appendix: Key Concepts and Glossary	25
Understanding Key Concepts	25
Additional Key Concepts	26
j. p. ames	28
About the author	28

Understanding 365/Azure for Everyone

Chapter 1: Introduction to Microsoft 365 and Azure

What are Microsoft 365 and Azure?

Microsoft 365 Microsoft 365 (formerly Office 365) is a suite of cloud-based productivity tools designed to help individuals and businesses collaborate and communicate more effectively. It includes popular applications like Word, Excel, PowerPoint, Outlook, Teams, and OneDrive.

Azure Azure is Microsoft's cloud computing platform, offering a wide range of services for building, deploying, and managing applications and services through Microsoft-managed data centers. Azure provides services such as virtual machines, databases, storage, networking, and more.

Benefits of Cloud Services

- **Scalability**: Easily scale resources up or down based on your needs.
- **Cost-Effectiveness**: Pay only for what you use, reducing capital expenditures.
- **Accessibility**: Access your data and applications from anywhere with an internet connection.
- **Security**: Benefit from robust security features and compliance with industry standards.

Difference Between Microsoft 365 and Azure

Microsoft 365 is primarily focused on productivity and collaboration tools, designed to enhance communication, document management, and teamwork. It includes applications and services like Outlook, Teams, OneDrive, and SharePoint.

Azure, on the other hand, is a cloud platform that provides infrastructure, platform, and software services. It supports a wide range of scenarios, from hosting websites and applications to managing databases, machine learning, and Internet of Things (IoT) solutions.

Real-World Use Case: Choosing Between Microsoft 365 and Azure

Imagine a small business owner, Sarah, who needs to improve her team's collaboration. She chooses Microsoft 365 because it offers tools like Teams for communication and OneDrive for file sharing. On the other hand, John, a software developer, needs a platform to host his web application. He opts for Azure because it provides virtual machines and databases necessary for his project.

Chapter 2: Setting Up Microsoft 365

Domain Assignment

What is a Domain? A domain is a unique name that identifies a website or an email address on the internet (e.g., yourcompany.com).

Assigning a Domain to Microsoft 365

1. **Log in to the Microsoft 365 Admin Center**

   - Access the admin center at <u>admin.microsoft.com</u> and log in with your admin credentials.

2. **Navigate to the Setup Page**

   - Go to `Setup > Domains`.

3. **Add Your Domain**

   - Click `Add domain` and enter your domain name (e.g., yourcompany.com).
   - Follow the prompts to verify your domain ownership. This typically involves adding a TXT record to your DNS settings.

4. **Verify Domain Ownership**

   - Log in to your DNS provider's management console.
   - Add the provided TXT record to your domain's DNS settings.
   - Return to the Microsoft 365 Admin Center and click `Verify`.

5. **Complete the Setup**

   - Follow the remaining prompts to complete the domain setup, including configuring your email addresses and other services.

Real-World Example: Setting Up Your Company's Email

Imagine you run a small business called "Tech Solutions" and you want to set up professional email addresses for your employees. You own the domain techsolutions.com. By following the steps above, you can assign this domain to your Microsoft 365 account, allowing you to create email addresses like john.doe@techsolutions.com and jane.smith@techsolutions.com.

Chapter 3: Active Directory Integration

What is Active Directory (AD)?

Active Directory (AD) is a directory service developed by Microsoft for managing and organizing a network of computers, users, and other resources. It allows administrators to manage permissions and access to network resources.

Azure Active Directory (Azure AD) Azure AD is the cloud-based version of Active Directory, providing identity and access management for Microsoft 365 and other cloud-based applications.

Benefits of Active Directory Integration

- **Centralized User Management**: Manage user accounts and access permissions from a single location.
- **Single Sign-On (SSO)**: Users can access multiple applications with one set of credentials.
- **Enhanced Security**: Implement security policies and controls across your organization.

Integration with Microsoft 365 and Azure AD

1. **Set Up Azure AD Connect**
   - Azure AD Connect is a tool that synchronizes your on-premises Active Directory with Azure AD.
   - Download and install Azure AD Connect from the Microsoft website.
2. **Configure Synchronization**
   - Follow the setup wizard to configure synchronization settings, including selecting which organizational units (OUs) and attributes to sync.
3. **Enable Single Sign-On (SSO)**
   - Configure SSO to allow users to sign in to Microsoft 365 and other cloud applications with their on-premises credentials.

Real-World Example: Centralized User Management

Imagine you manage a growing company with multiple departments. Each department has specific applications and resources they need access to. By integrating your on-premises Active Directory with Azure AD, you can centrally manage user accounts and permissions, ensuring each department has access to the resources they need while maintaining security.

Table: Benefits of Active Directory Integration

Feature	Benefit
Centralized Management	Simplifies user and access management from a single interface
Single Sign-On (SSO)	Users access multiple applications with one set of credentials
Enhanced Security	Enforces security policies across all connected applications
Improved Productivity	Reduces the time IT spends on password resets and access issues

Chapter 4: Conditional Access Policies

What are Conditional Access Policies?

Conditional access policies are a set of rules that determine how users can access your organization's resources. These policies use signals such as user location, device state, and application sensitivity to enforce access controls.

Benefits of Conditional Access Policies

- **Improved Security**: Protect against unauthorized access and data breaches.
- **Flexible Access Controls**: Implement access controls based on specific conditions and requirements.
- **Compliance**: Ensure your organization meets regulatory and compliance requirements.

How to Create and Manage Conditional Access Policies

1. **Access the Azure AD Admin Center**
   - Log in to the Azure AD admin center at aad.portal.azure.com.
2. **Navigate to Conditional Access**
   - Go to `Security > Conditional Access`.
3. **Create a New Policy**
   - Click `New policy` and give it a name.
   - Define the conditions for the policy, such as user or group, cloud apps, and conditions like location or device state.
4. **Configure Access Controls**
   - Choose the access controls to enforce, such as requiring multi-factor authentication (MFA) or blocking access.
5. **Enable and Review the Policy**
   - Enable the policy and review its settings to ensure it meets your security requirements.

Real-World Example: Restricting Access Based on Location

Imagine you want to enhance the security of your company's data by restricting access to Microsoft 365 applications based on user location. You create a conditional access policy that blocks access from outside the country where your company operates. This ensures that only users within the approved geographic location can access sensitive data.

Table: Example Conditional Access Policy

Condition	Action
User Location: Outside Country	Block Access
Device State: Unmanaged Device	Require Multi-Factor Authentication (MFA)
Risk Level: High	Require Password Change

Chapter 5: Two-Factor Authentication (2FA)

Integrating 2FA with Microsoft 365

What is Two-Factor Authentication (2FA)? 2FA is an additional layer of security that requires users to verify their identity using two different methods, typically something they know (password) and something they have (a mobile device).

Benefits of 2FA

- **Enhanced Security**: Protects against unauthorized access even if passwords are compromised.
- **Compliance**: Meets regulatory requirements for data protection.

Setting Up 2FA with Duo and Other Providers

1. **Enable Multi-Factor Authentication**
    - Log in to the Microsoft 365 admin center and navigate to `Active users`.
    - Select the users you want to enable 2FA for and click `Manage multi-factor authentication`.
2. **Choose an Authentication Provider**
    - Microsoft 365 supports various 2FA providers, including Duo, Google Authenticator, and Microsoft Authenticator.
    - Follow the provider's instructions to set up 2FA for your users.
3. **Configure User Settings**
    - Users will need to complete the 2FA setup process by linking their mobile device or other authentication method.

Real-World Example: Securing User Accounts with 2FA

Imagine you run a law firm and want to ensure that sensitive client information is protected. By enabling 2FA for all employees, you add an extra layer of security to their Microsoft 365 accounts. Even if an employee's password is compromised, the attacker would still need the second factor (e.g., a mobile device) to gain access.

Table: 2FA Providers Comparison

Provider	Features
Duo	Easy integration, push notifications, biometric
Google Authenticator	TOTP, QR code setup, widely supported
Microsoft Authenticator	TOTP, push notifications, seamless integration

Chapter 6: Mail and Licensing

Setting Up and Managing Email

Configuring Mailboxes in Microsoft 365

1. **Create User Accounts**
   - Log in to the Microsoft 365 admin center and navigate to `Users > Active users`.
   - Click `Add a user` and enter the necessary information, including the user's email address.
2. **Assign Mailboxes**
   - Assign an Exchange Online license to the user to create their mailbox.
   - Configure mailbox settings, such as email aliases and forwarding rules.
3. **Manage Email Settings**
   - Use the Exchange admin center to manage email settings, including spam filters, retention policies, and mailbox permissions.

Managing Licenses and Subscriptions

1. **Access the Billing Section**
   - Navigate to the `Billing` section in the Microsoft 365 admin center.
2. **Purchase and Assign Licenses**
   - Purchase the necessary licenses based on your organization's needs.
   - Assign licenses to users, ensuring they have access to the required Microsoft 365 services.
3. **Monitor Usage**
   - Regularly review license usage to ensure you are not over- or under-licensed.
   - Adjust your subscription as needed to match your organization's requirements.

Real-World Example: Allocating Licenses to Users

Imagine you manage a team of 20 employees, and each employee needs access to email, Microsoft Teams, and OneDrive. You purchase the appropriate Microsoft 365 licenses and assign them to each user, ensuring they have access to the necessary tools for their job.

Table: Common Microsoft 365 License Plans

License Plan	Features Included
Microsoft 365 Business Basic	Email, OneDrive, Teams, web versions of Office apps
Microsoft 365 Business Standard	Email, OneDrive, Teams, desktop and web Office apps
Microsoft 365 Business Premium	All features of Business Standard, plus advanced security and device management

Chapter 7: Virtual Servers and Storage in Azure

Creating and Managing Virtual Servers

What are Virtual Machines (VMs)? Virtual machines (VMs) are software emulations of physical computers. They run an operating system and applications just like a physical computer but are hosted on a physical server.

Setting Up Virtual Machines in Azure

1. **Log in to the Azure Portal**
   - Access the Azure portal at portal.azure.com and log in with your credentials.
2. **Create a New Virtual Machine**
   - Navigate to `Virtual Machines` and click `Create`.
   - Select `Azure Virtual Machine` and choose a configuration template or start from scratch.
3. **Configure the VM**
   - Enter the required details, including the VM name, region, and resource group.
   - Choose the operating system, size, and disk type.
4. **Networking Settings**
   - Configure the networking settings, including the virtual network (VNet) and public IP address.
5. **Review and Create**
   - Review the configuration settings and click `Create` to provision the VM.

Managing Virtual Machines

1. **Access VM Settings**
   - Navigate to `Virtual Machines` and select the VM you want to manage.
2. **Start, Stop, and Restart**
   - Use the control options to start, stop, or restart the VM.
3. **Monitor Performance**
   - Use the monitoring tools to track CPU, memory, and disk usage.
4. **Update and Patch**
   - Regularly update the operating system and applications to ensure security and performance.

Real-World Example: Hosting a Website on Azure

Imagine you are a web developer who needs to host a client's website. By setting up a virtual machine on Azure, you can easily deploy the website, configure the necessary resources, and manage the server remotely. This provides a scalable and cost-effective solution for hosting web applications. **Table: Azure VM Sizes and Use Cases**

VM Size	Use Case
B1s (Basic)	Development/testing, small web servers
D2s_v3 (Standard)	Medium-sized applications, SQL databases
F8s_v2 (Compute optimized)	High-performance computing, large-scale databases

Chapter 8: SharePoint and File Management

Why Ditch a File Server for SharePoint?

Benefits of Using SharePoint

1. **Security**
    - SharePoint offers robust security features, including encryption, access controls, and compliance with industry standards.
2. **Accessibility**
    - Access files from anywhere with an internet connection, improving collaboration and productivity.
3. **Automatic Archival**
    - Automate the archival of documents, ensuring important files are preserved.
4. **Auditing**
    - Track and audit user activities, ensuring accountability and security.
5. **2FA Capability**
    - Enhance security with two-factor authentication (2FA) for accessing sensitive documents.

Real-World Example: Migrating Files to SharePoint

Imagine your company relies on a traditional file server that is difficult to manage and requires regular maintenance. By migrating to SharePoint, you can simplify file management, enhance security, and provide employees with easy access to documents from any location. This transition reduces IT overhead and improves efficiency.

Table: SharePoint vs. Traditional File Server

Feature	SharePoint	Traditional File Server
Security	Encryption, access controls, compliance	Basic permissions, less robust
Accessibility	Anywhere with internet	Limited to local network
Automatic Archival	Yes	No
Auditing	Detailed user activity tracking	Limited
2FA Capability	Yes	No

Chapter 9: Teams and Collaboration

Using Microsoft Teams for Collaboration

Setting Up Teams for Your Organization

1. **Log in to the Microsoft 365 Admin Center**
    - Access the admin center at admin.microsoft.com and log in with your credentials.
2. **Navigate to Teams and Groups**
    - Go to `Teams & groups` > `Teams`.
3. **Create a New Team**
    - Click `Create team` and choose a team type (e.g., private, public).
    - Enter the team name and description.
4. **Add Members**
    - Add team members by entering their email addresses.
5. **Configure Team Settings**
    - Configure team settings, including permissions, channels, and tabs.

Integrating Teams with Other Microsoft 365 Services

1. **Add SharePoint Libraries**
    - Integrate SharePoint libraries into Teams for easy file access.
2. **Use OneNote**
    - Add OneNote to Teams for collaborative note-taking.
3. **Schedule Meetings**
    - Use the Teams calendar to schedule and manage meetings.

Real-World Example: Organizing Team Communication and Projects

Imagine you manage a project team that works remotely. By using Microsoft Teams, you can create dedicated channels for different aspects of the project, share documents via SharePoint, collaborate on notes with OneNote, and schedule virtual meetings. This integration streamlines communication and improves project management.

Table: Microsoft Teams Features and Benefits

Feature	Benefit
Channels	Organize conversations and projects
SharePoint Integration	Easy file access and sharing
OneNote Integration	Collaborative note-taking
Meetings	Schedule and manage virtual meetings

Chapter 10: Power BI and Data Visualization

Getting Started with Power BI

Introduction to Power BI Power BI is a business analytics tool that allows you to visualize data and share insights across your organization. It enables you to create interactive reports and dashboards.

Creating Reports and Dashboards

1. **Log in to Power BI**
   - Access Power BI at powerbi.com and log in with your Microsoft 365 credentials.
2. **Connect to Data Sources**
   - Connect to various data sources, including Excel, SQL Server, and Azure.
3. **Create a Report**
   - Use the drag-and-drop interface to create visualizations, such as charts, graphs, and maps.
4. **Build a Dashboard**
   - Pin visualizations to a dashboard to create a comprehensive view of your data.
5. **Share Insights**
   - Share reports and dashboards with your team to collaborate and make data-driven decisions.

Real-World Example: Visualizing Sales Data with Power BI

Imagine you are a sales manager who wants to track the performance of your sales team. By using Power BI, you can create interactive dashboards that display key metrics such as sales revenue, target achievement, and customer acquisition. This enables you to identify trends, make informed decisions, and present data to stakeholders effectively.

Table: Power BI Features and Use Cases

Feature	Use Case
Data Connections	Connect to various data sources (Excel, SQL, Azure)
Visualizations	Create charts, graphs, and maps
Dashboards	Build comprehensive views of your data
Sharing	Collaborate and share insights with your team

Chapter 11: Networking and Security

Local Networking Integration via IKE VPN

Setting Up IKE VPN to Connect LAN to Azure

1. **Log in to the Azure Portal**
    - Access the Azure portal at portal.azure.com and log in with your credentials.
2. **Create a Virtual Network Gateway**
    - Navigate to `Virtual Network Gateways` and click `Create`.
    - Configure the settings, including the gateway type, SKU, and virtual network.
3. **Configure the Local Network Gateway**
    - Set up the local network gateway with your on-premises network information.
4. **Create a VPN Connection**
    - Establish a VPN connection between the virtual network gateway and the local network gateway.
5. **Configure the On-Premises VPN Device**
    - Set up your on-premises VPN device to establish the IKE VPN connection with Azure.

SSLVPN Capabilities and Their Importance

1. **Secure Remote Access**
    - SSLVPN provides secure remote access to your network over the internet.
2. **Encryption**
    - SSLVPN encrypts data transmitted between the user and the network, ensuring data privacy.
3. **Ease of Use**
    - SSLVPN is user-friendly and can be accessed from various devices, including laptops, smartphones, and tablets.

Real-World Example: Securely Accessing Azure Resources from Your Local Network

Imagine your company has critical applications hosted on Azure, and employees need secure access to these resources from the office. By setting up an IKE VPN, you can establish a secure connection between your local network and Azure, allowing employees to access Azure resources as if they were on the same network. Additionally, SSLVPN enables remote employees to securely connect to the network from anywhere.

Table: IKE VPN vs. SSLVPN

Feature	IKE VPN	SSLVPN
Secure Remote Access	Yes	Yes
Encryption	Yes	Yes
Device Compatibility	Limited to configured devices	Wide compatibility
Use Case	Site-to-site connectivity	Remote user connectivity

Chapter 12: Additional Crucial Features

Other Important Features of Microsoft 365 and Azure

Azure Functions and Automation

- **What are Azure Functions?**
    - Serverless computing service that allows you to run code without managing infrastructure.
    - Ideal for automating repetitive tasks and building event-driven applications.
- **Setting Up Azure Functions**
    - Create a new function app in the Azure portal.
    - Choose a template and write your code.
    - Set up triggers and bindings to automate workflows.

Microsoft Intune for Device Management

- **What is Microsoft Intune?**
    - Cloud-based service for managing devices, apps, and security.
    - Ensures compliance and protects data on both corporate and personal devices.
- **Setting Up Intune**
    - Log in to the Microsoft Endpoint Manager admin center.
    - Configure device policies and profiles.
    - Enroll devices and manage app distribution.

Real-World Example: Automating Routine Tasks with Azure Functions

Imagine you manage a large e-commerce platform that needs to send daily sales reports to the management team. By setting up an Azure Function, you can automate this task, generating and sending the report at a specified time each day. This saves time and ensures consistency in reporting.

Table: Azure Functions vs. Traditional Servers

Feature	Azure Functions	Traditional Servers
Infrastructure Management	None (serverless)	Required
Cost	Pay-as-you-go	Fixed cost
Scalability	Automatic	Manual
Use Case	Event-driven, automated tasks	General-purpose computing

Chapter 13: Case Studies and Best Practices

Real-World Case Studies

Case Study 1: Small Business Migration to Microsoft 365

- **Background**: A small consulting firm with 50 employees needed to improve collaboration and reduce IT costs.
- **Solution**: Migrated to Microsoft 365, implementing Teams for communication, SharePoint for document management, and Power BI for data analysis.
- **Results**: Increased productivity, improved collaboration, and reduced IT overhead.

Case Study 2: Enterprise Adoption of Azure

- **Background**: A large manufacturing company required a scalable solution for their global operations.
- **Solution**: Adopted Azure for hosting critical applications, using virtual machines, databases, and Azure Functions for automation.
- **Results**: Enhanced scalability, reduced downtime, and improved operational efficiency.

Best Practices for Implementation and Management

1. **Plan and Assess**
   - Conduct a thorough assessment of your current infrastructure and business needs.
   - Develop a clear migration plan with defined goals and timelines.
2. **Train and Educate**
   - Provide training sessions for employees to familiarize them with the new tools and services.
   - Offer ongoing support and resources to address any issues.
3. **Monitor and Optimize**
   - Regularly monitor usage and performance to identify areas for improvement.
   - Optimize resource allocation to ensure cost-efficiency and scalability.

Table: Best Practices for Microsoft 365 and Azure Implementation

Best Practice	Benefit
Plan and Assess	Ensures a smooth migration with clear goals
Train and Educate	Empowers users to effectively use new tools
Monitor and Optimize	Maintains performance and cost-efficiency
Regular Updates	Keeps systems secure and up-to-date

Appendix: Key Concepts and Glossary

Understanding Key Concepts

MAC Address

- **Definition**: A unique identifier assigned to network interfaces for communications on the physical network segment.
- **Real-World Example**: Like a fingerprint for your network device, uniquely identifying each device on your network.

IP Address

- **Definition**: A numerical label assigned to each device connected to a computer network that uses the Internet Protocol for communication.
- **Real-World Example**: Like the street address of your house, telling other computers where to find you on the internet.

DNS (Domain Name System)

- **Definition**: The phonebook of the internet, translating human-friendly domain names into IP addresses.
- **Real-World Example**: Like a phonebook, converting names into phone numbers (IP addresses) so you can make a call.

Ports

- **Definition**: Doors and windows of your house, allowing different types of data to enter and exit your network.
- **Real-World Example**: Different doors for different purposes, like a front door for guests and a back door for deliveries.

Vulnerability (CVE)

- **Definition**: A flaw or weakness in a computer system that can be exploited by a threat actor.
- **Real-World Example**: Like a weak lock on your door, making it easier for burglars to break in.

Two-Factor Authentication (2FA)

- **Definition**: An additional layer of security requiring two different methods to verify identity.
- **Real-World Example**: Like using both a password and a fingerprint to unlock your phone.

Additional Key Concepts

CVE (Common Vulnerabilities and Exposures)

- **What is a CVE?**
    - A list of publicly disclosed cybersecurity vulnerabilities and exposures.
    - Each CVE is assigned a unique identifier for easy reference.
- **Why CVEs are Important**
    - Identifying and understanding CVEs help in protecting systems against known vulnerabilities.
- **How to Subscribe to CVE Alerts**
    - Visit the CVE website and subscribe to their mailing lists for updates.

CISA (Cybersecurity and Infrastructure Security Agency)

- **What is CISA?**
    - A U.S. government agency responsible for enhancing cybersecurity and infrastructure security.
- **Why CISA Alerts are Important**
    - Provides timely information on cybersecurity threats and vulnerabilities.
- **How to Subscribe to CISA Alerts**
    - Visit the [CISA website](#) and sign up for email alerts.

Remediating a CVE
- **Identify the Vulnerability**
    - Use CVE and CISA alerts to identify relevant vulnerabilities affecting your systems.
- **Assess the Risk**
    - Determine the severity of the vulnerability and its potential impact.
- **Apply Patches**
    - Check if a patch is available from the vendor and apply it promptly.
- **Implement Mitigations**
    - If a patch is not available, implement temporary mitigations to reduce risk.
- **Monitor and Verify**
    - Monitor your systems to ensure the vulnerability is effectively addressed.
- **Document and Report**
    - Document the remediation process and report the actions taken.

j. p. ames

About the author

Mr. Ames is a four-decade computer scientist who has traveled the world for his work. Living near New York City for more than 30 years, he speaks Spanish and enjoys writing books on a diverse range of topics including romance, science fiction, history, pop culture, artificial intelligence, quantum physics, spy satellites, classic television and travel photography. Mr. Ames is an FCC licensee, also certified in virtualization and advanced firewalls. His hobbies include collecting coins, fluorescent and phosphorescent minerals, Amateur radio and enjoying time outdoors with his wife and children as well as studying historic computer operating systems. His business, Cartoon Renewal Studios, employs Artificial Intelligence to restore, upscale and colorize historic films and cartoons.

www.ingramcontent.com/pod-product-compliance
Lightning Source LLC
Chambersburg PA
CBHW072057230526
45479CB00010B/1126